No, Smoke!

by Logan O'Brien
illustrated by Marilyn Janovitz

Practice Decodable 16

McGraw Hill Education

Bothell, WA • Chicago, IL • Columbus, OH • New York, NY

MHEonline.com

Send all inquiries to:
McGraw-Hill Education
8787 Orion Place
Columbus, OH 43240

ISBN: 978-0-02-145056-5
MHID: 0-02-145056-0

Printed in the United States of America.

8 9 10 CTM 23

Can Smoke run out?

Smoke pokes his nose out.

No, Smoke! No!

Smoke runs and runs.

Rose makes a note.

Rose tapes it on a pole.

A boy sees the note.

The boy sees Smoke.

Smoke is home!